FROM THE LIFE OF A GANGSTER TO

A TROPHY OF GOD'S MARVELOUS GRACE

THE AMAZING TRUE LIFE STORY

FRANKIE PALERMO

AS TOLD TO CHUCK KENNEDY

NBM

NO BOUNDARIES MINISTRIES

A TROPHY OF GOD'S MARVELOUS GRACE
Copyright © 2013 Frank Palermo
No Boundaries Ministries
Printed in 2013

Library of Congress Catalog Number: 1-911099558

ISBN: 978-0-578-12299-1

All scripture quotations are taken from the King James Version.

PUBLISHED BY:
No Boundaries Ministries
PO Box 14931
Bradenton, FL 34280

DISTRIBUTED BY:
No Boundaries Ministries
PO Box 14931
Bradenton, FL 34280

International Prison Ministry
PO Box 2868
Costa Mesa, CA 92628

Book cover and design by Shahn Flood, International Prison Ministry
Book interior layout by Heidi Ceballos, International Prison Ministry
Printed in the United States of America

Acknowledgments

First and foremost I dedicate this book to my beautiful wife Judy. Through her love and devotion these past 17 years, she continues to motivate and inspire me in this ministry we share together.

I want to thank our beloved Pastor, Chuck Kennedy, for his spiritual guidance and precious friendship to this ministry. Our heart-felt thanks to him for the many hours spent in the writing of this testimony. Without him this book would not be possible.

I want to thank Lori Hudson for her many hours of transcribing my testimony from a DVD to a manuscript on paper.

I want to also thank Belinda Keys for her many hours spent editing and correcting grammar.

And to our dear friend J. David Stephens, Second Assistant General Overseer, Church of God International Offices, for the kind words: "I have known Frankie and Judy Palermo for many years, witnessing their dynamic evangelistic ministry first hand. They are the real deal. As authentic and anointed servants of the Lord Jesus Christ, they share His good news with a compelling and relative voice. I recommend them highly as committed and qualified ministers of the Gospel."

We have changed some of the names in this book for legal reasons.

Table of Contents

	Acknowledgements	3
Chapter 1	**Shoot Out at the Corral**	7
Chapter 2	**With God All Things Are Possible**	17
Chapter 3	**Meet My Grandmother**	21
Chapter 4	**A Big Time Gangster Like My Dad**	29
Chapter 5	**Initiation Into the Mob**	37
Chapter 6	**A Life of Crime**	47
Chapter 7	**Men of the Bomb**	55
Chapter 8	**On the Run**	63
Chapter 9	**The Arrest**	75
Chapter 10	**My Heavenly Visit in Hell**	85
Chapter 11	**Bible College**	93
Chapter 12	**My Beautiful Wife Judy**	99
Chapter 13	**The Life of an Evangelist**	107
Chapter 14	**Closing Thoughts**	117

For the gift and calling of God are
without repentance.
—Romans 11:29

●

Chapter 1

Shootout at the Corral

He lunges toward me with a knife, two other guys right behind him. Things progressed so quickly it is hard to describe exactly how it all happened. Bang! Bang! Bang! Before I knew it, the gun was out of my holster, and I had put two bullet holes into the knife-wielding man. The third shot took out his buddy behind him. The last guy started screaming and running in the other direction. Good thing he dove behind the bar when he did, or that final shot would have splattered his brains everywhere.

The girl who had caught my eye was taking cover somewhere on the other side of the room. She was just screaming and crying as both her friends lay clinging to life in a pool of blood on the floor.

Everyone is in total shock. Andy is behind the bar looking at me with his mouth open, while others are shaking and fearing for their lives. Then Andy turns to me and says, "Get out, get out of here." Quickly I moved toward the door, glancing around the Corral, and pointing my pistol at anything that moved. Fortunately, they were all taking cover, or things would have gotten uglier. I ran to my car, jumped in it, and took off to my hide out.

What brought me to Lansing, Michigan, originally, was a guy by the name of Jimmy "the Pro" McLaughlin. Jimmy "the Pro" was a safe cracker. There was not a safe he could not crack. That's what earned him the nick name "Pro," because he was the best at unlocking a safe. I called Jimmy "the Pro" and told him what had happened. I was seeking his expertise in what to do next. He picked me up immediately, and said the first thing we had to do was to get rid of my car. We took it to a place called Petie's Auto Body, also known as Petie's Chop Shop. This place was well known amongst the mob for making cars disappear. He had a machine there that would crush them beyond any recognition. So Petie crushed my Chevy and made it disappear, license plate and all.

In the meantime, we contacted Dominic "Fats" Aleo, who was an under boss in the mafia. Jimmy knew him very well and was able to solicit his help on my behalf. Now Fats was about 5'5", bald headed and

SHOOTOUT AT THE CORRAL

he weighed about three hundred pounds. The last person that called him "Fats" to his face got a whiskey bottle broken over his head and ended up needing a long stay in the hospital. Fats had a reputation as being a killer.

To get me out of Lansing, Dominic Fats Aleo made arrangements to transport me to Cleveland, Ohio, and from there to Philadelphia. I was driven by an associate of the mob by the name of Jimmy Brown. At the time of my arrival in Cleveland, John Scalisi was the boss of the crime family in that city. Once in Cleveland, I met with his under boss to make arrangements to get to Philly. While this was taking place, I called my cousin Louie and he informed me how the news had picked up the story, and a search was on to find out who this Jerome Clibbanoff was.

Louie told me I had more serious problems than that, however. He said the family had summoned me to a meeting, and he was not sure what was going to happen when I got there. He was not even sure I would come out of that meeting alive. No matter what though, I had better show up.

Phil Patelli and Carmine Grasiano, who were made members of the mafia in Philadelphia, were scheduled to be involved. After arriving in Philadelphia, I was to notify Louie, and he would notify them to get the time and location. I did not know what was going to happen at this meeting, but I knew I was in big trouble. Louie also informed me there was going to be another guy who would come, but he did not know who it was. Now I was even more uncertain that if I went in, I might not come out alive. I did not have a choice. If I did not show up, it was a certain death sentence.

The order was, "Do not get in trouble," and I had disobeyed that order from the mob. "Stay away from anything that might bring the police," they told me, and I had walked right into a major high profile case with me being the center of attention. This was not good. The next order I had broken was not to use any firearms. "Don't be shooting people or killing anyone. You are being proposed as a made member of the Boston family and are not allowed to do anything that will bring Federal heat on the family." Those were the orders, and with the Corral shooting I had disobeyed them. My life was on the line.

The meeting was called at 12th Street and Washington Avenue in a Mafia member's house by the name of Leo Masso. It was a very nice house set up for entertaining, with a bar in the basement and a jukebox containing a variety of popular tunes. Louie drove me to the meeting. He was very concerned for my life, because he knew how upset they were with my behavior. Not to mention the reputation I was starting to acquire.

Louie and I walked into the meeting, and Phil was there with Carmine. Maybe a half hour later, Paul "the

Waiter" Ricca shows up from Boston. He was one of the captains of the family in Boston. Paul was at this meeting because he was the one who proposed me to become a made member of the family in Boston.

I was shocked to see him, to say the least. He pulled me aside with a hug and a kiss advising me rather sternly, "Whatever you do, don't say anything. Keep your mouth shut. Don't argue with nobody. Don't try to make yourself out to be right, just humble yourself so you will live."

We continued to wait for the main guy to show up. We waited and waited. Had a few more drinks and waited. I had no idea who this was going to be. Suddenly, there was a knock upstairs on the door. Then the mystery man we had been nervously waiting for started down the cellar steps. The minute I heard him coming down those stairs, it was as if I froze like an ice cube. I was petrified not knowing what was to happen next. As he got in sight, I was astounded. It was none other than my father, the Boss of the Philadelphia mob, and he was mad. I turned white as a sheet when I saw him, because I knew what was coming next. He came marching on down those steps and he was cursing left and right. I mean he turned the room blue, frothing at the mouth, screaming and yelling at me. Phil and Carmine were trying to calm him down, telling him, it is ok, we would talk it out, and he was screaming, "No, it's not ok!" Then he went to pick up a chair to hit me with it. He had a vicious temper. So he grabbed a bar chair to hit me while Phil and Carmine tried to restrain him. Then Paul "the Waiter" stepped in and pulled my father aside for maybe fifteen or twenty minutes. Paul had a way with Dad. Tensions eased, and then the two of them returned. My dad had calmed down. Paul instructed me to tell him my side of the story, exactly as it had happened. I was very respectful in my tone of voice and proceeded to explain to Dad the how and why of the shooting at the Corral.

The Corral was a bar I used to frequent located on the east side of Lansing, Michigan. It was near the University of Michigan State where I befriended several students and dated some of the girls while party hopping with the guys. Many a night I would crash at one of the dorms when I could not make it to my own place a little ways outside of town. I was about twenty-five years old at the time and frequented the Corral on a somewhat regular basis. The bartender was named Andy, and he knew me only as Jerome or Jerry Clibbanoff, an alias due to my criminal history. I was already a fugitive wanted for various crimes, so I was forced to adopt an alias identity which I had stolen from someone unknown to me.

Never unarmed, I carried a pearl handled .32 colt special snub nose in a shoulder holster and kept a .32 caliber Derringer pistol strapped to my back just in case. Usually I never had any problem in the Corral. I would just enjoy a few drinks with some music, dancing, and sandwiches in the company of my friends while having a good time.

I explained to Dad that this particular night I was at the bar enjoying a few drinks, five to be exact, but I did not tell that part to my Father. "Wild Turkey" was my drink of choice, which is a hundred proof drink. After my fifth Wild Turkey, I was not drunk, but somewhat relaxed. In walk three guys with a very lovely lady. She was possibly in her early twenties. Two of the guys had a rugged demeanor about them and the third was ordinary. But the girl was very beautiful to look at, and clearly in the company of these three men.

They sat at the bar just down the way from me, and I happened to glance in their direction while they were getting settled in. The young lady looked my way and our eyes met; she smiled and so did I. My thoughts were repetitive, "Wow, she is so beautiful, what a girl!" Andy stepped over and interrupted my fascination with her by starting some small talk while serving me another Wild Turkey.

Pretty soon, the three men called for the bartender. Andy started mixing them drinks as the lovely lady glanced my way again. My eyes met hers a second time. She smiled, and I smiled back. At this point her boyfriend picked up on our mutual attraction and said something to her that I was unable to hear. Next he turned around to me angrily and started railing me with words like, "What do you keep smiling about you blankity-blank Italian?" He was cursing at me and spewing slang names at me. I turned in his direction while thinking to myself, "What is wrong with this guy?" Then I looked him in the eye and said, "By the way, I am not Italian, I am Jewish." "Oh," he says, "you are one of them dirty Jews then," still trying to pick a fight with me.

Ignoring him again, in an effort to stay out of trouble, I quietly went back to my Wild Turkey. Problem was, he just would not give up. He gets louder and moves closer to me saying, "You keep staring at my woman. What is it, do you want my woman or what? Do you want a piece of her, is that what it is?" I looked back at him and calmly replied, "Look buddy, I don't want any trouble with you, but if trouble is what you are asking for, I will give you all you want."

They quickly pushed the girl out of the way while the other two stepped up with the mouthy one and moved very close to me. With his left hand he pulled out a a six-inch knife like a switchblade, waving it in my face and proclaiming, "I am going to carve your blankity-blank face up like a Christmas turkey." I could tell he planned to make good on his threats.

I was ready, though. Years of practice in drawing my gun had made me confident to do what I needed to do without a second thought. Even to this day I can shoot the caps off of bottles at twenty to twenty-five yards, and my eyesight is not what it used to be. Whatever I aimed for I would hit. Bang! Bang! Bang! I stopped the man with the knife, Dad, what else could I do?

I told my dad I had no choice, it was self defense, and he just sat there what seemed like an eternity before he looked at me and said very seriously, "You are one lucky boy tonight, son. That you are going to walk out of here alive shows you are one lucky boy. But let me make it clear, if there are any more incidents with you and guns and killing people, believe what I am saying to you, son, you are going to be like one of them, DEAD."

Louie and I, along with everyone else in that room, knew he meant it, because that was the way we lived, on the edge. Thanks to Paul "the Waiter" Ricca, tensions eased, and Paul even started telling some jokes about some of the Mafia guys and everyone was laughing. Louie and some of the others nicknamed it the OK Corral, like the movie, and Louie said I was Doc Holladay. We joked and carried on, but I knew I had dodged a bullet that night myself.

So I did put away the .32 snub nose special that I had been carrying, but I kept the Derringer on my back just in case. Wisdom says, "Never take a knife to a gunfight." Afterward, I headed for Boston to become a made member of the Mafia and make a name for myself just like my father.

Chapter 2

With God All Things Are Possible

I thank God nobody died at The Corral that night. Both men survived the gunshot wounds. Only the man who was pulling the trigger, Frankie "D" Palermo, died later. I am not referring to a physical death, but I was crucified with Christ: never the less I live; yet not I, but Christ lives in me.

This is my life story. It is not pretty or pleasant for the most part, at least until I got saved. But it is how I actually experienced God's wonderful grace and love on a personal basis. These are the intimate details of my story. How God touched me and changed my life forever. The point of this testimony is to assure all who read it, that if God can change a gangster like Frankie "D" Palermo, He can change anybody! Jeremiah 32:17

boldly proclaims, "Ah Lord GOD! Behold, thou hast made the heaven and the earth by thy great power and stretched out arm, and *there is nothing too hard for thee*." Again in Mark 10:27, Jesus said that with men these things are impossible, but *with God all things are possible*. We are talking a changed heart here. Only God has the power to reach down into the soul of man and change his inner desires. That is what He did for me. The impossible being His specialty.

My testimony is a clear example of God's power to change even the worst of the worst. The beautiful thing is that His love has no boundaries. It is available to whoever will open their heart and receive.

Within this book there is hope for everyone. Included are the most depraved and degenerate men, once written off as having no hope. Even if the worst murderer, the worst rapist, and the worst of the worst of this world were to give their heart to Jesus, regardless of what they have done, there is enough room at the cross, and enough power in the blood, to forgive such a one! The natural mind cannot comprehend it. But my life story herein is living proof that *there is nothing too hard for God*. I miraculously now stand as one of many, a Trophy of God's Marvelous Grace!

The scripture that has been the basis of my personal testimony for all of these years is found in the first chapter of Galatians, verses 10-12. "For do I now persuade men, or God? or do I seek to please men? for if I yet pleased men, I should not be the servant of Christ. But I certify you, brethren, that the gospel which was preached of me is not after man. For I neither received it of man, neither was I taught it, but by the revelation of Jesus Christ." It was by revelation that I received this gospel while alone in my cold, dark federal prison cell, and I am saved today because of it.

I am a recipient of the supernatural revelation of Jesus Christ in that He literally saved and changed my life. You see, I should be dead. You don't know how many times men have tried to kill me. I really should be dead and in hell. Even after I was saved and released from prison, there have been five attempts on my life.

I still get threats against me today, and at this book's writing I am in my late 70's. I made a lot of enemies along the way. You don't know how many have been hurt. I was involved in some despicable crimes, and even though I repented and got saved, many whom I hurt have not. Most are dead now.

I often think on these things through the years. Especially August 27, 1971, when I gave my heart to Christ over 40 years ago. On that night I met Jesus, King of kings and Lord of lords, in person. Mafia member Frankie "D" Palermo died and was born again a new man. This had to be a supernatural act of Jesus. I cannot express with words just how grateful I am. But as you read my testimony, I pray you will see why.

Chapter 3

Meet My Grandmother

I was born and raised in Philadelphia. There I attended Catholic school all my youthful years. I never knew the love of a mother; in fact, I never met my mother. Dad divided up me, my brother and sisters between various relatives, and I was sent to live with my grandmother.

She had come to Philly from the island of Sicily in her native country of Italy. She could not read, write, or speak a bit of English. I went to live with her when I was five years-old, and so, of course, I had to learn at a very young age to speak her native Italian tongue in order to communicate. I can still speak it pretty good today. Grandma died when I was 14 years-old, and I was not sad when she did. Let me explain why.

My father was a powerful man. He controlled the Philadelphia Mob from 1940 to 1962. No one dared disturb him lest they lose their life. As I mentioned, I never knew my real mom. My grandmother raised me. I do not know if she just hated the fact that she was forced to raise me, or if she was just mentally deranged. Whatever the case, I was the object of her perverted abuse for the next nine torturous years.

Sad to say, she forced me to spend all those youthful years like a caged animal. Grandma locked me alone in the cellar, night after night, in the pitch dark, where she tormented me on a continual basis with fear and beatings. In her sick mind, I was no better than a dog, so she would feed me from a dog's dish.

She would beat me severely with a cane, regularly and mercilessly. I was made to drink water from the toilet bowl, and frightened by tales that the werewolf would get me. She would go so far as to dress in a sheet and come down the cellar stairs at night just to hear me scream in utter fear. She was a master of manipulation with fear. I remember many nights she would take a rake and scrape it on the cellar windows in the black of night. You can imagine the horrible noise piercing the otherwise silent evening. It would have frightened any adult, much less a pitiful, motherless young boy being held captive as a prisoner alone in the basement afraid for his life. She thrived on control by fear, and I was the direct object of it.

Other relatives knew what was going on, but they were too afraid of my dad to say anything. No one dared breathe a word to the powerful Mafia Boss about it. He never knew of the torturous crimes she committed against me until after her death.

All the while as a young man growing up in this sadistic atmosphere, I was being programmed by Satan to hate and fear. I feared the dark, I feared being alone, I feared what each new day would bring. This abuse built an intense anger and hate inside me. That is not to be reasoned as an excuse for the things I later did, but it was certainly a motivating evil force in my life.

Just to show you the emotional condition I was in, at age fourteen I could not tie my shoelaces alone, my brother would tie them for me. After my grandmother died, I was brought up out of the cellar and my aunt moved in to care for me. She brought my brother and three sisters with her. Things were better with her, but the damage had already been done.

I was an angry young man. I loved boxing, so I took up the sport. However, the anger showed in my boxing. There was a man down the street named Charles Worth that had a punching bag in his garage. Me and some of the other neighborhood kids used to go there and work out after school. He was a big help in training me. He was also the one who suggested I get involved in the Germantown Police Athletic League not too far from where I lived in Philly. Since Grandma was dead and Dad was not around, I told my aunt and she said maybe we should let Dad know. But we never did.

I ended up winning the featherweight championship. Most of the boys in this league are one hundred and twenty-six pounds. Due to my past, I weighed in at only one hundred and twelve pounds. I took on much bigger guys with forty-eight total fights, and won forty-seven of them. The one I lost was to a Mexican kid who was quite a bit older than me. Many trainers and managers suggested that I go professional, but I was too young. I did try to get a license but was refused at every place. To be professional, you had to apply with the Pennsylvania Athletic Commission or the New Jersey Athletic Commission. All of them turned me down once they heard my Palermo name, son of "Blinky" Palermo. They would not touch me because of my father's career, so that ended my boxing aspirations.

Before I met the Lord, I followed the Catholic church with all its rituals. It was all I knew. I remember as a young man while attending Catholic school, I used to go to confession. One time in particular I went into the confessional booth, and it was dark in there. You can't see the guy on the other side, and I was supposed to tell him my sins. Once completed, the priest said to me, "Son, I want you to come back here in two weeks, and I'm going to grant you absolution of the church." Well, I felt like a dummy because I had never heard that word before. So I leaned up a little bit more in the dark booth, trying to see the priest on the other side, and I said, "Father, uh Father, what was that word? Did you say solution, solution-what?" He replied in a very syrupy religious tone, "Ab-so-lu-tion." Hmmmm, I curiously inquired, "What exactly does that mean?" "Forgiveness, it means forgiveness for your sins," the priest said. "In the meantime though, I want you to recite the rosary, the Our Father, the Glory beads, and do the novena in the church." Now I'm thinking to myself, "What? What is happening here?" A little stunned, I reluctantly agreed, "Okay, father," and I quickly got out of the confessional and went outside. Now I will never forget this. I was pacing up and down outside that Catholic church and saying to myself, "I went into this church upset about the things I have been doing and looking for help, but now I come out of the church in worse shape than when I went in!" Religion kills while a relationship with Jesus sets you free. But I was unaware of it at that time.

Later I was properly taught the Word of God while attending Bible College. They taught me that there is only one mediator between God and man. It is not a Catholic priest. It is not the Pope. It isn't even some evangelist or pastor. There is only one mediator between God and man and He sits at the right hand of God making intercession for us all. His name is Jesus, and He is the only one who can forgive sin. Thank God

I learned that early on, because it has been my point of reference many times throughout the years.

Frankie (standing) and Fred (Frankie's brother)
as young lads. Frankie is five years old.

The house on 64th Street in Philadelphia, PA
Frankie's grandmother confined him to the cellar as a young boy and
tormented him with harsh punishments and fears.

Frank "Blinky" Palermo (center, squatting) with Abbott and Costello.
Frankie is behind his father in the white sports coat.
Top row, two men are bodyguards.

Chapter 4

A Big Time Gangster Like My Dad

Shortly after being released from prison, I found myself at one of the family houses where I had been tortured by Granny. It was a mansion. I remember eleven bedrooms upstairs, several more downstairs, a four car garage, and more. But I hated it. I hated it because of the tormenting memories I had while I was held captive there. My hate took action in the form of arson. I poured gasoline from top to bottom of this hell hole called home and burned it to the ground.

Grandma had long been dead, but I thought somehow I could burn up those memories of the evil that had taken place there all those years. Instead, I realized I had turned out to be a big time gangster just like my dad.

While growing up, that was my desire, to be a big time gangster like my father. He controlled the Philadelphia mob until retiring in 1962. He was such a very powerful man throughout the 40's and 50's, and I wanted to be just like him. He reigned as boss over syndicated crime in Philly until he retired. Actually, I very seldom saw him, but I continuously heard about him on television, radio and the newspapers. I thrived in my vain imagination when hearing sensational talk of how he deviously controlled, and I would think to myself, "Oh boy, I am going to be just like my dad."

My heart's hope all those younger years was to be a gangster just like him. Sad to say, I never had a real relationship with him. I would only get to see him once in a while when he would come to the house. Grandma would clean me up and bring me out of the basement to make everything look normal while he was there.

Love was never mentioned in our house. Throughout my life, I never once heard my father tell any one of my siblings that he loved us. We just never heard that. The only thing I knew was that my father controlled the powerful mob, and I wanted to be more powerful than he was. I was consumed by this evil inner drive.

Dad ended up dying in a Philadelphia hospital at the ripe old age of 91. He wasn't shot down like many of the other mobsters he was associated with. He was not pushed in a trunk or shoved in a barrel and tossed in the sea like the fate of many I knew. Actually, my dad died in the hospital at the age of 91 due to a stroke.

Let me make it very clear again, that I never had a relationship with my dad at any time in his life. After my salvation experience in prison, it even got worse. He actually cut off all communication with me once I met the I Lord. I was quickly barred from the family. He was acutely aware that I carried my Bible now instead of a weapon. He heard about me in prison preaching the word of God and afterward refused all contact with me. He would not see or speak to me. I was informed by his body guards at the house that I was not welcome anymore, and if I knew what was good for me I had better stay away from him permanently.

I am sharing with you about my dad because he was a powerful man and made quite an impression on me, even from a distance. One of his most well known enterprises was a fight manager. He was a boxing promoter with Don King and some of the others. He had five world champion boxers that he managed, including heavy weight champion of the world, Charles Sonny Liston. It was Mohammad Ali who took the title off of Liston in Lewiston, Maine, with the phantom punch. I won't say too much about that because I'm still friends with the Ali family today. However, the sum of it was that Dad had five world champions with all the fame and fortune that goes with it, including plenty of money and vacation homes in various places like Miami and others. But at the time, I was still a prisoner in Grandma's basement having nothing to do with any of it. The knowledge of all this was fuel for fire inside me to become the big time gangster just like my dad. Only problem was, sad to say, it was all in my head. I only knew Dad from a distance.

Educated as a youth in Catholic school, we had a nun who was our teacher by the name of Sister Mary Frances. There were about thirty kids in our class. One day she gathered us all together and made us form a circle. She told us to stand up one at a time and tell all the class what we wanted to be when we grow up. I was the last one to get a turn, and all of these kids stood up before me and told how they wanted to be a lawyer, a doctor, a fireman, and so on.

Well, it was all so beautiful, and everybody was clapping every time one of the children would get up and say what they were going to be when they grew up. The guy right before my turn was named Leonard, little Leonard we called him. He stood up and proudly proclaimed, "When I grow up, I will join the Northwest Mounted Police." Boy, did everybody start clapping and yelling, because he was going to wear the red and blue pants with the hat, and he was going to be in the Mounties! Next it was my turn. Sister Mary Frances said, "Master Francis, would you stand up and tell us what you want to be when you grow up?" I stood up just as bold as I could in front of that whole class. I will never forget looking at everybody, sticking out my chest, and saying, "When I grow up, I want to be a big time gangster, just like my father!" You could have heard a pin drop! Nobody clapped; nobody yelled. It was silent, dead silent. Everybody was stunned and did not know quite what to do. Then Sister Mary Frances sternly looked at me, grabbed me by the ear, and marched me down to the principal's office to see Mother Marie.

Reach back in time with me here. Back then it was common to give you the ruler, pull your hair, smack you, or even more. There was no such thing as calling 911. Forget about that, because 911 was not even around yet. I wound up down in Mother Marie's office and she said to me, "Okay big shot! Is that what you want to be? A gangster, do ya?" Well I got the knuckle treatment with the ruler instead, if you know what I mean.

Then she said to me, "I'm going to write a note to your grandmother. You take this note home and give it to her." I made her think I had every intention of being an obedient child. I definitely took the note home to my grandmother.

However, remember my grandmother couldn't read English. I went home with the note alright, and I gave it to Grandma. She studied the note for a few minutes, and in Italian she said, "What does this mean? What's this all about?" I said, "Ma, the school said they're very proud of me, and I'm a very good boy!" She did not know any better and congratulated me. I learned to lie for my benefit at a very early age. My goal was to be a big time gangster, just like my father, and I was on the way.

My father was well known. He made Life Magazine in 1952 with five other Mafia men. Many times he made the Philadelphia Daily News, but one particular article at his death was titled, "Blinky Palermo's Passing Marks the End of Terror in Philadelphia." There were other photos in various publications regarding when gangsters ran boxing, like the photo with the caption, "Mafia Man Okay to Gamble in Atlantic City."

Let me explain a little about that situation. It was about the time casinos first came to Atlantic City. The game commission scoped out all of the Mafia heads in the country, complete with pictures, and instructed their security people not to allow these gangsters in the casinos. Well, my father being who he was, went into Resorts Casino, if I remember correctly. Security immediately grabbed him, escorted him out with the directive to not come back again, telling him he was barred from there, and to stay away.

My father did something nobody else did. He took them into federal court. Amazing as it may sound, he actually went into federal court and won! Upon returning victorious to the same casino, they gave him

$100,000 in chips, and anything he wanted was on the house!

For his 75th birthday, he had a big party at a well known night club. All of my family was present but me. With my three sisters and my brothers' arms around him celebrating his 75th and having a grand ole time, he refused to let me be a part. I was unable to even wish him a happy birthday. That's the way he wanted it, and that's the way it was. You did not argue with my father without dire consequences.

Later, while Dad was on his death bed, my brother Freddy was able to go see him. He could just barely talk because he was dying. He called my brother closer to him, and laboring to talk or breathe, gasping for breath, he whispered, "Is Frankie still preaching?" My brother leaned down and said, "Yes, yes, Frankie is still preaching." With a blank stare, my father just looked at Freddy and never said another word. This was the last thing Dad said before he died. Then he just slipped on into eternity. I am still not certain why he asked Freddy that question. Speculation at best is all I can do. I won't know until I cross over whether Dad was glad for me in his dying breath, or if he still hated me because of my call to preach. The Mafia has a saying to those who are not one of them. You treat us good, we will treat you better. You treat us bad, we will treat you worse.

Chapter 5

Initiation Into the Mob

People do not realize how vicious the mob is. They see them portrayed on television and movies, so they think they know, but in reality they have no idea how terribly ruthless, murderous, and vicious they really are. I know because I saw some of the methods they would use, and for the most part they are too bad to mention. Take for example, one of the ways they extract information from those who don't want to talk. They bind you with cords and take an electric drill up your nose. You will talk, I assure you. Or maybe they will put it through your eardrums, convincing you really quick to give up the information they want. They have methods that you would not believe, ones that normal people never even think of. A ruthless machine without feeling, yet in human bodies. How does one get that far gone? A little at a time. It starts a little at a time with wrong desires and an unquenchable thirst for power.

One example was a bookmaker and loan shark by the name of John Marelli. He began to do some betting on the side and ended up losing some of the mob's money. He was stealing anywhere from five to six thousand dollars a week from the family. Now if you steal the mob's money, it is an automatic death sentence. They summoned him to come for a meeting similar to the one they had called me to, but he never came out. When he went into the meeting to explain where all the money had gone and what had happened, they tied lassos around his neck. The Mafia calls this the rope trick. One guy holds on one end, and another guy holds on the other end, and they would proceed to tug and pull until they literally pulled the life out of him, like the tug of war from hell. All because he had dared to cheat the mob out of their money. Greed has a price to pay. You just do not steal from the mob, either within or without; it is an unbroken rule that John learned the hard way.

As ruthless and vicious as they are, the mob is a family, a brotherhood, if you please. There are rules that are understood with each family member. For instance, you do not touch any other made member's family or children. In fact, you better not touch an-

other made member at all. If there is a dispute between two members, it is to be brought before the
commission and never handled between each other. If
you touch another family member, no matter which
city they reside in, you will die. It is just that simple.

The commission decides who is right and wrong,
and what the just punishment will be. They decide who
is going to die, and who is going to live. That is the way
it is in the mob. Violations to this are fatal. There are
many other rules and regulations involved, but I am
mentioning these so you will understand the bond of
brotherhood and how the organization works.

Another practice is called the oath of "omerta," and
that means that you take the oath of silence. In other
words, you take an oath, backed by your life, to be
blind, deaf and silent, so that you will live a long life. It
is an old Sicilian custom, to know nothing, to see nothing, and to hear nothing. This is the law of the mob,
otherwise you die.

My initiation into the "family" happened on the
north end of Boston, Massachusetts, at Hanover and
Commercial Street. I believe the year was 1957, but it
has been so long ago I could be mistaken. At that time
Raymond Patriarca was yet to become the most powerful New England Mafia boss. He hailed from Rhode
Island, and we were good friends. We used to have
lunch together quite often. He was Boston, Maine,
New Hampshire, Rhode Island and Connecticut's most

powerful Mafia boss ever. People still talk about him in this day and age. However, he was not the boss at the time I was being introduced into the family.

Here is how the hierarchy works in the mob family. First of all, you have the boss, who is the boss of the entire family. Whether it be Philadelphia, Chicago, New York, or whatever territory he reigned over. There is only one boss in each family, period. Then you have an under-boss, who is directly under the main boss. After that is the consigliere, who is also called the counselor of the family. He is the adviser in disputes. He must have a good knowledge of the family first and foremost. He actually acts similar to an attorney, but he is not a lawyer. The captains are next. The "caprigenie" they call him, which means captain. The captain has a crew. You may have eight or ten captains in a family, and every captain has a crew that consists of anywhere from ten to fifteen guys that are Mafia members, whose job is to go out and earn money. This can be anything from loan sharking, robbing, stealing, extortion, bribery, counterfeiting, or whatever way they can earn money to sustain the family. Members of the crew are called soldiers. Every single day they must report to the captains everything they do; it is very important.

Now when you take this oath into the family, you know you must live up to it, or you are going to die. That is what it means to be La Cosa Nostra, which translates "our thing," or A Miga Nostra, which translates "our family together." These names mean you are a part of a very secretive society.

First of all, when you are called to become a member, you must prove your loyalty. You work directly under your caprigenie, or captain. You first need to make your bones in order to become a member. This is terminology that means you are willing to kill for the family, or you are willing to help in killing for the family.

My captain at the time I was to become a made member was a guy by the name of Paul Ricca, of whom I was doing some work for only as an associate of the mob. The term "made member" means you have become one of the Family. An associate is one who does work for the Family, but is not a member. In order to be become a made member, you must be proposed for membership. Once approved and initiated, you are then a made member for life.

Another thing about the mob is everyone gets a nick name. Paul Ricca was known as Paul "the Waiter" Ricca, because he used to be a waiter before he was in the mob. So he was called Paul "the Waiter" Ricca. Now don't be thrown off by his nick name; he was one tough guy. When he gave an order, you had better obey it, regardless, let me assure you of that.

My nick name was Frankie "D." I was given that for the middle name I used to be known by. The "D" stood for dunamis, or dynamite, thus they called me Frankie "D." That was long ago and under the blood. Now I am a child of King Jesus. Thank God all that is forgotten. Jesus is the only one I serve now.

The under boss at that time was a guy by the name of Frank "the Canadian" Messino, because he was from Canada. And the main boss at that time was Henry Noise. "Noise" was his nick name and his last name was Nardella. Henry Noise and I had a great relationship. I really liked Henry at the time. He got his nick name because he always made a lot of noise killing people. He was the boss, and you did not joke or play around with him.

Sometime in 1957, I was ordered to meet with my boss, Paul "the Waiter" Ricca, in North Boston. His orders to me stated that I should meet him the next day wearing a suit and a tie and looking real nice. He told me I was going to be proposed for Mafia membership in the family. I was excited. He further stated that when the boss asked me if I knew why I was there, my answer was to be "no". They did not want you to know you were going to be proposed as a made member of the Mafia. You were not supposed to know that in advance.

The next day I did as ordered and met Paul "the Waiter." I was so elated to become a member of this most powerful Mafia family. Later I would be transferred to the New York mob, but I was not aware of it at this time.

This all took place at Gero's Cafe, a beautiful Italian restaurant. They had a back room in the rear of this very upscale restaurant. I remember walking in with Paul "the Waiter," and he instructed me to go sit up front with the boss. There was a long head table where Henry was seated with maybe ten other men. Henry looked at me and said, "Frankie, sit down here." I took a chair beside him. He gave me that look, staring at me for what seemed to be an eternity. You just knew by that look that he meant business, and he was nobody to fool with.

His first question to me was, "Do you know why you are here?" I looked at him and replied, "No, I do not know why I am here." Then Henry asked me, "Do you know everybody here?" I looked around the table and said, "Yes, most all of them." He proceeded to ask me if I liked these people here, and I replied that I did, "Yes, Sir, I do." "Do you know that this is a brotherhood, a secret society?" was his next question. "Yes," I replied. He continued by telling me that in this brotherhood, or secret society, there is only one way in and only one way out. "There is no return from this. Do you understand this? None," he repeated. I said, "Yes, I do understand that the brotherhood is first and foremost in our life." He then looked sternly at me again for some time and said, "Would you kill for us?" My reply, "Yes, yes I would."

Then he asked me which finger I would use to pull the trigger with. I showed him my right index finger, and pointing it upwards, I indicated, "This one." Just then the underboss, Frank Messino, came over and told me to hold out my right hand. He then proceeded to take a needle and prick my finger with it until I bled. He then stated to me, "You are now blood of our blood, you are one of us."

I was then instructed to kiss Henry Noise on both cheeks, which I did. Then I was told to go around the room and shake hands with everyone that was there and kiss them on the cheek. I did that. When I returned back to my chair at the head table and sat down, everyone else stood up, all except me. They all joined hands together for what they term "tying the knot." Tying the knot meant we were then all one family together. Then Henry speaks up, "In honor of our brotherhood, I untie the knot." At that, everyone let go. He then spoke something in Italian that I did not understand. I was directed to stand. We formed a circle, all of us together, and Henry said in Italian, "In honor of our brotherhood, I tie the knot with our new brother!"

At this point I am tied in with them by holding hands with everybody in the circle. I am now one of them. Henry says to me that I am now a friend of theirs. This is the day I became a made member of the Boston Mafia, and later I would transfer to the New York Family to become a member of the Genovese Mafia crime Family.

Before leaving I was ordered to report to my captain everyday. I was to check with him. I could do nothing without him knowing about it. I was told I had to follow the chain of command. One last thing about this, they made it very clear to me that they had no allegiance to God or to any country, not even their own. The only allegiance we had was to this immediate family. Our wives, our children are secondary. La Cosa Nostra is first above everything and everyone from this day forward. He reiterated to me that if I wanted to believe in God, my country, my family, all is well and good, but that is to come after this family. If I did not obey all rules and regulations of the brotherhood, my fate would be death. They made it very plain to me that day.

Two others besides myself were inducted into the brotherhood that day, and then we sat down to a great Italian feast like you would not believe. So ended the day, and now I was La Cosa Nostra, just like my dad. I could do whatever I wanted to do because I had a powerful Mafia family behind me. I was officially one of them.

Chapter 6

A Life of Crime

All it takes is one suggestion from the enemy to get yourself in trouble, just a thought. You don't become a fornicator, a liar, an adulterer, a cheater, or a murderer, until first it begins in your heart. It's like what Jesus said in Matthew 15:11, "Not that which goeth into the mouth defileth a man; but that which cometh out of the mouth, this defileth a man." He is saying that out of the abundance of the heart, or what you think on, your mouth speaks. Then James tells us in Chapter 3, our tongues are the rudder that steers our life. What we think comes out in words, and then our words become actions, and our actions tell it all.

What I am saying is that if you take a thought the enemy gives you and meditate on it until it drops into your heart, you will eventually act on the enemy's suggestion, and end up in a world of trouble. I knew nothing about this man called Jesus. I didn't know anything about being saved or being born again. I never heard of those kind of things growing up. Today I know. You must be born again, that's the bottom line.

I'll tell you how I first began a life of crime. I was walking by the bank one day, and I heard a voice speak to me. Some would say, "Oh, Brother Frankie, you really heard a voice?" You better believe I heard a voice; it was like a whisper. This is what I heard: "You know how easy it would be to rob that bank?" Well, I accepted that evil thought, and within a week I committed my first felony. I robbed that bank.

Then I moved into counterfeiting. We had suitcases filled with counterfeit money in increments of $50 and $100 bills and would sell them for twenty cents on the dollar out of New York. Graduating to interstate transportation, stolen securities, stocks and bonds, I continued to go deeper and deeper into the criminal lifestyle. Forgery, burglary, armed robbery; you name it, I did it.

My cousin Louie and a couple of other guys joined up with me along the way. Louie and I sat down at one point and tried to figure out how much money we had made together. It was over a couple of million dollars each. Problem was we had nothing to show for it. What I am telling you is Satan will take you on a roller coaster ride making you think it's never going to end, but it does. There is a pay day coming one day. That is the law of God.

We were doing a bank job up in Pittsburgh. Myself, Louie, Freddy Harrison, and a guy by the name of Frank Jenkins, four of us total. It was about 9:30 in the morning, and we planned to hit this bank really quickly. In and out was the plan. Louie was to cover the entrance of the bank with a shotgun, I would go down the center, Freddy and Frank Jenkins would jump over the counters and get the money. Once we entered, we all started screaming, "This is a hold up!" All the customers and employees just froze and stood shaking, not knowing what to expect. We pointed our weapons at them and shouted, "Down on the floor, now!" Freddy and Frank jumped over the counters and began to rake the money into the bags. I was standing in the center watching if anybody moved, or if someone might come in. Louie was guarding the back, ready to throw down on anyone entering from the rear.

Everything was going as planned. Everyone got down and there was no shooting. Freddy and Frank Jenkins were grabbing the money, and we were right on schedule. We had a three to four minute window to execute all this and then get out. We were doing it until, all of a sudden, a little elderly man walks in. He does not even notice Louie, he just walks right on past him. This little old man is carrying a cigar box in his hands. He must have been in his eighties. Louie yells at him, "Hey you, hey you, stop! Throw that box down and lay down on the floor, do it now!" The little old man turned around and just stared at Louie, it was like he froze or something. Louie lifted the shotgun up and moved toward him. Now Freddy, Frank Jenkins and myself stopped in mid-stream, and our eyes were quickly moving from the little old man to Louie and back, not knowing what was about to happen.

All eyes moved to Louie and I am thinking to myself, please Louie don't shoot, don't shoot Louie. I did not know what Louie was going to do because I know Louie, and I was sure hoping he would not hurt the elderly man.

Instead of throwing the box down and falling on the floor like Louie was telling him to do, he defiantly started walking right into Louie's shotgun that was pointed at him. He came within maybe three feet of that shotgun barrel while Louie was yelling, "Get down, get down! Give me that box!" The little old man refused to do so. He just turned around and melted to the ground on his knees, clutching that box securely to his chest with both arms as if in a praying position. He then fell on over face first with the box still underneath him. Since he was down, Louie stopped yelling and moved away from him, thank God.

By this time Frank Jenkins and Freddy had collected the money in the bags, about thirty-four thousand dollars I think it was, and so we started toward the back exit. We told them nobody was to get up if they wanted to live. Then we made our getaway. We were all running out the door, and Louie was the last one out of the bank. I heard Louie saying to the little old man, "I don't know what you got in that cigar box, but it sure wasn't worth your life over it, Mister."

We never found out what he had in the box. All imagining is just guess work, but it was important enough for him to risk his life for it. We got away clean for the moment. I was so thankful Louie did not shoot that man, because not only would he have needlessly lost his life, but I would have been charged with murder.

Louie is dead now. I loved him dearly. We were close because we did so much together. Thank God for Judy, my beautiful wife, because Louie called one day and he said to her, "I'm at the end of the road and I don't know what else to do with my life. I'm just so disgusted with it that I feel like taking my own life." Judy said, "Louie, I want to meet you. Let's meet somewhere." He agreed, and they met at a prayer tower in Long Beach, New Jersey. That is where Judy led him to Christ.

You know what he did after he got saved? He got up in front of the church and testified that he was a new person in Christ. I thank God I know my cousin is in heaven now, and I look forward to seeing him again when I get there.

Now you must understand where Louie came from to really appreciate this. His mob nickname was Louie "the Pipe." This is what he was called because he was an enforcer for the mob. He always carried a 12-inch piece of steel pipe which he used on his job. He thought nothing of cracking you on the head to get the job done. But now he is forgiven, hard as it may be for the mind to comprehend. The grace of God reached down and turned Louie "the Pipe" into a saint of God! What a mighty God we serve!

I met some guys out of New York, and they invited me to New York City so they could introduce me to some of the big mob guys up there. There are five major crime or Mafia families in New York City. People often ask me, "Are they still there?" Yes, they never left. They are still there. You knock out ten of them, and ten more step up. No one can break them. Today they are even more vicious and ruthless, because of the younger generation of guys that are coming up in the mob. The wise guys, as they are known, or la cosa nostra. They are still there, trust me.

Around the end of the 50's, I went to New York City. My godfather is dead now, so I can say his name, Vincent Gigante. He took over the Genovese crime family when Don Vito Genovese died. Don Vito died in the Atlanta prison. After his death, Gigante "the Chin" took over. They called him "the Chin." No one ever mentioned his real name. If you ever talked about Vincent Gigante, you never said his name. You would just grab your chin as a signal or sign. If you were talking to another member of the Mafia, he would know exactly who you were talking about when you touched your chin. He knew it was Gigante without you ever having to say his name.

He became my godfather, and I loved him dearly. The reason I loved him was because he protected me. Even after he knew I had met the Lord in prison, he said to me, "If you ever have trouble when you get out of prison, you send word to me. Ain't nobody gonna hurt you." But I had somebody greater than Gigante, I had the Lord Jesus Christ on my side. That's why Brother Frankie is still alive.

Chapter 7

Men of the Bomb

There was a war out in Youngstown, Ohio, in progress. Several mob guys in Youngstown were fighting for control of the Ohio mob. They were killing people left and right. There had already been about ten murders preceding my arrival. Cleveland was having trouble, so they sent word to New York to get some help out there. These guys were killing one another. "Men of the bomb" they called it, because people were getting blown up with car bombs. I was sent out there along with a couple of others. Before it was all over, I was accused in three murders and a million dollar arson. I was now a big time gangster just like my father.

There was a tough guy by the name of Vince "the Prince" Janairo. He owned the Prince spaghetti house, and thus his nickname, Vince "the Prince." It was a beautiful Italian restaurant with great food. Well, he declared himself to be the new boss of Youngstown, Ohio. He had a beautiful blue convertible Buick, and as he was leaving his restaurant in the morning hours, he got into his car. When he cranked it, the car blew up. The impact of the explosion sent him flying through the convertible roof and onto the street. His right arm was completely severed from his shoulder. The news media reported this on the next day and showed a picture of his severed arm laying in the street with his hand open. Somebody from the mob had placed two meatballs in the severed hand. That was the message the mob was sending to Vince "the Prince" Janairo, you are nothing but a meatball. You are not running this organization of the crime family here. This was how they were eliminating the ones who tried to take over as the boss.

Next were the Naples Brothers, Joey and Sandy Naples. I remember this well. Joey Naples' doorbell rang, and when he answered it, a shotgun blast went off. The blast not only killed Joey by entering his stomach and passing on through, but killed his girlfriend that had been standing behind him as he answered the door.

Now the mob has a rule that you do not kill innocent people. Only if they are an enemy or a danger to the family, are they to be eliminated. You do not kill to just kill. This girl had no business being murdered, except that she was in the wrong place at the wrong time, standing directly behind Joey when he opened the door. Sad to say, the blast ripped out his intestines and continued its deadly assault right into the girlfriend, killing them both instantly. Joey had also made the fatal mistake of announcing he was going to be the boss of the area.

Next, his brother Sandy stepped up and proclaimed that he would take over where Joey left off. That did not go over very well, and in short order he was murdered while he was in his car. I am not sure where he was going that evening, but he had stopped on the road along the way when two men came out of the bushes with shotguns and literally blew him to pieces. He lay dead in the street like several of his predecessors.

Then came Rocko Rocky Callvalaro, who stood up and said he was in control of the mob now. He made it very clear he was in control of Cleveland and also Youngstown, Ohio. This murder involved the unfortunate death of two young children. He was going to his office one morning around 8:30 or 9:00 am. He was heading to his car, and his little nine-year-old son was with him. While they were getting into the car, a neighbor boy from across the street asked if he could have a ride to school. Rocky obliged the young man, not knowing what was about to happen. He told him to hurry up and climb into the back seat. I personally had no knowledge whatsoever that someone from the mob had planted a bomb under Rocky's car. Furthermore, the ones who planted the bomb had no idea he would be transporting two children that morning, as there were consequences behind that killing. I cannot go into that, but suffice it to say that the ones responsible had consequences from the mob for killing two innocent children.

When they were all in the car and ready to go, he turned the ignition and the bomb blew the car up. Callvalaro was killed instantly. His son in the front seat was killed instantly. The young man in the back seat was paralyzed for three weeks in the hospital before he died.

There were two informers for the FBI who accused me of being in Youngstown, Ohio, right around Thanksgiving when this happened. I was in town, but I repeat, I had no knowledge of the planned murder of this man whatsoever. I am explaining why the FBI issued warrants for me for the Callvalaro murder.

The two informants, however, were sentenced to life in prison for cutting a guy's throat in Cleveland and dumping him out of the eleventh floor of the hotel window. An undercover cop caught them coming out of the hotel, and they were arrested, later convicted, and given a life sentence. The FBI suspected I was involved, so they issued warrants for me from Nevada to the east coast. I got some kind of sadistic thrill out of all the attention and the hunt. I was a well known gangster like my dad, and now everybody knew who I was. This is what I wanted, to be just like my dad. I thought that was great. That is the way I thought. Crazy as it may seem, my thinking had become so twisted that those were my exact thoughts when it took place.

Bad things happened out there, very bad things. People lost their lives. Like the situation I described involving the kids that mistakenly got caught in the ambush by the car bomb and died. Eventually, a man named John Orzo successfully took over the family and put an end to all the killings. I was still a highly sought after, wanted man all over the country, with the FBI pursuing me diligently. With forty-eight agents from the FBI commissioned to Youngstown to clean it up, I was put on the run.

The charge of arson against me came about the time when the agents came into Youngstown with a program called Ban the Bomb. It was a council that met to do away with the bombings that had been happening. The council met in a bank building, which ended up being burned to the ground, where the Ban the Bomb council were trying to stop all the murders. It was a million dollar building now in ashes, and I was the prime suspect. This is where I was accused of committing arson and was issued a subsequent warrant for that as well. Later, I was brought to trial in front of Magistrate Kider on this charge, but never convicted. I was now hot on the run trying to evade the investigators and agents who were pursuing me.

Frank "Blinky" Palermo shaking hands with Thomas Mitchell, who played the angel in "It's a Wonderful Life." Top row, left to right: Cappy Hoffman, Willie Wiseberg, and Barone.

Frank "Blinky" Palermo's 75th birthday
From left to right: Rosa, Emma, Violet, and Fred.
Frankie was not permitted to attend the event, as his father had rejected him after his conversion.

Chapter 8

On the Run

My brother had a Jewish deli in Philadelphia, Pennsylvania, across from the Sheraton Inn. I needed to get out of Ohio, so I went back to Philly and checked into the Sheraton across from my brother's place. He had a nice deli near the University of Pennsylvania where the college kids used to come eat his delicious corned beef, Swiss, pastrami and rye, bagels, and more.

I was across the street at the bar drinking my troubles away inside the Sheraton. Augie was the bartender, and I knew him well. It was getting close to eleven that night, and I decided to get in touch with my cousin Georgie. So, I went around the corner of the lobby, found a phone booth, closed the door, and placed a call to him. Now Georgie was a pretty tough guy. He was into labor racketeering and some other things of the same nature. Over the years, Georgie and I had done a lot of private work together. We had a great relationship.

All of a sudden, Georgie starts laughing right in the middle of our conversation. A little annoyed at him laughing, I said, "Georgie, what are you laughing about?" I was talking serious business, and I did not appreciate that he thought it was funny. "What are you laughing at, Georgie?" I demanded. Still chuckling, he replied, "Frank, you are on television, yeah, you are on the eleven o'clock news right now! There you are! You look good, Frankie! Ha Ha!"

"Get out of here, Georgie," I retorted. "I don't have time for games." "Yep," he said. "Got your picture on TV right now. They want to talk to you about murder and a million dollar arson job in Youngstown, Ohio." I still was arguing with him in unbelief, when all of a sudden, Augie came tapping the glass of the phone booth urgently. While Georgie was holding the phone, I opened the door to see what Augie wanted. "You are on the news, Frankie, you are on the news! You better get out of here fast. Too many people know you," Augie whispered in a frantic tone.

He quickly put my change from the bar into my hands and signaled me to get out by another exit instead of going back into the bar again. I thanked Augie and told him I would make sure he was taken care of.

Then I bid farewell to Georgie and immediately left the hotel to go into hiding.

For maybe a week I hid out at another friend's home in South Philadelphia. Then I decided it would be best for me to head towards upstate New York. Buffalo was appealing, because it was controlled by the Maggadino family. At that time the sons, Stefano, or Steve, Maggadino and Nino Maggadino, were in control. Their dad had a funeral home there. They were a very powerful Mafia family in their day with control of both Buffalo and the Erie Pennsylvania areas.

Sam Ragatore was in the vending machine business, but he worked for the Maggadino family. I made a phone call to him explaining my situation. He wanted to know how I was going to get up there. I told him by Greyhound Bus to Erie, PA. It was April and still snowing a little, so I asked him to arrange for somebody to meet me at the bus stop in Erie and take me on over to Buffalo.

He mentioned a kid by the name of Billy Markazie that I had met sometime back, but never really had any dealings with him. He assured me Billy would be there for me when I arrived. I was not aware that Billy Markazie had been busted a few times and was now planning to trade me to the FBI so they would drop his charges.

It was cold and snowing as I boarded the bus and headed towards Erie, PA. I remember two kids sitting in front of me. I am so thankful today I had packed my gun in my luggage below. If I would have had it, this story might have ended here.

Anyway, we were disembarking, and the two boys were playing as boys do with their mom telling them, "Come on now, boys, come on." I remember looking around at everything, wondering about all the big wooden yellow crates I saw. As I took a step down off the bus, Billy Markazie dressed in his large trench coat and hat, came running up speaking in Italian. It is translated "I don't know nothing." "I don't know nothing! What's going on here? What is going on?" Never dreaming it was a set up, I was looking at him wondering, "What did he mean, what is going on here? What is he trying to tell me?"

All of a sudden, six armed FBI agents ran out from behind these crates and jumped me. My hand was in my pocket clutching my handkerchief since I had a terrible cold at that time. They were screaming at me, "If you pull anything out of your pocket, you are a dead man!" They threw my arms behind me and cuffed me within a few seconds. Then they placed me under arrest for arson on the Ban the Bomb bank building and suspicion of murder. Billy disappeared, never to be seen again.

I was transported to Grove City, Pennsylvania, where I was held in the jail there for three days before I could get a hearing. The Magistrate in Grove City was named Magistrate Kider. Around 11:30 pm, a guard taps on my cell. "Are you awake, Frank?" I said, "Yeah, yeah, I am here." He said, "Somebody wants to talk to you on the telephone. I need you to come with me." "Listen, Sarge," I retorted in my rebellious tone, "I don't know nobody here. Why would I get a phone call? I don't want to talk to nobody." I actually thought it was a set up or some sort of trap.

He insisted that if I hear the voice, I will want to talk to this person. Reluctantly, I agreed and he escorted me handcuffed downstairs. I picked up the phone and immediately recognized the voice on the other end. It was my dad. He first asked if I was alright and then wanted to know one question. "Did Billy Markazie set you up?" he sternly inquired. "Dad, I don't really know. I was to meet him there, but I don't know what happened. It was all so fast," I replied. "All I know is that he was supposed to pick me up at Erie and take me into Buffalo. The next thing I know the FBI were arresting me there." Dad said that was all he wanted to know and promised to send me help in the form of an attorney, Bob Gabriel from Philadelphia. He also said he would keep his distance from me due to the circumstances and informed me he would not be back in touch with me.

A couple days later I went before Magistrate Kider, and Bob Gabriel was there just like Dad had promised. There were also about ten FBI agents in the room along with the U.S. Attorney. They were there to convince Magistrate Kider that I should be sent back to Youngstown, Ohio, to stand trial for suspicion of murder and a million dollar arson.

Magistrate Kider asked them for evidence against me. Their reply was that they had two witnesses that could testify to my being in Youngstown at the time of the murder and arson. He informed them they would have to produce those two witnesses to testify in front of him in Grove, Pennsylvania, before he would send me back to Ohio. Hearsay testimony was not good enough to ship me back to Ohio. There must be hard core evidence.

The U.S. Attorney argued that this was impossible since the witnesses were incarcerated in Ohio with life sentences. These were the two men I mentioned earlier, caught by the undercover cop after they slit the guy's throat and splattered him on the street by tossing his body from the eleventh floor of the hotel.

Magistrate Kider was not impressed and demanded they be produced to testify in person against me, or I would go free. Again, the argument was reiterated that if these two convicted criminals were brought across the state line, they did not have to go back, thus they could not produce them to testify. This was the way the laws were at this time, so it just was not possible.

In the meantime, my attorney, Bob Gabriel, called the FBI agents to the witness stand, and one by one asked them, "Did you ever see Frank Palermo in Youngstown, Ohio, or do you have any personal knowledge he was there?" One by one they all answered the same, "No." "No." "No."

Since I was being held on a fifty thousand dollar bond, Magistrate Kider told them he would only hold me one more week in order to give them time to produce the two witnesses. Again the U.S. Attorney argued that it would be too difficult, and Magistrate Kider told them they had no choice or the case would be dismissed for lack of evidence. He repeated to them that there would be no extradition to Ohio on say so, there must be hard evidence.

A week later I was brought back in before the magistrate and the U. S. Attorney. They were unable to produce the two witnesses, and so I was dismissed of the charges. The attorney spoke up and said, "Your Honor, Mr. Palermo has a forgery check charge against him in Philadelphia, so I ask the court to retain him on that charge." He informed the Magistrate that there were agents scheduled to pick me up on that charge the next day and transport me back to Philly. The judge agreed to hold me 24 hours, or I would go free.

The next day, two detectives flew in from Philadelphia to take me back on the forgery charge. They planned to fly me back to face the judge there. I did not know these two detectives, but it seemed they had heard of me. As we were driving to the airport, one of them said to the other, "Hey, Larry, be careful what you say around this guy 'cause he will plant a bomb in your car and blow you and your family up."

We arrived at the airport and boarded Allegheny Airlines. They sat us in the front, near to where the cockpit is. Of course, I was handcuffed and in my coat because it was still cold. The stewardess began making her rounds to pass out barf bags. When I reached out to take one, she saw the handcuffs on me. Somewhat stunned, she started asking the detectives questions. They explained to her how I was a fugitive being transported back to Philadelphia for trial. Next thing I knew, here came the pilot, the Captain of the plane. He informed us we must go back into the terminal. We are not allowed to fly handcuffed. They must find other means to transport me back to Philadelphia. They were not happy about that!

We ended up at the train station with an eight hour train ride back. They were really not happy. On the train they took one of my cuffs off and placed it on the agent sitting beside me. I asked, "Why all this over a five hundred dollar check forgery charge?" Their reply was that they knew the kind of people I was associated with. They thought the mob would ambush the train in order to help me to get away. I tried to tell them that was not going to happen, but they did not believe me.

The forgery charge was dismissed once we arrived back in Philly when I went before the judge. I walked out a free man. However, it did not take long for the FBI to find out about all the other charges in Nevada, the shooting in Michigan, and the other crimes from across the country of which I was suspected.

Knowing this, I headed down to Miami Beach to hide. One night a whole bunch of us guys from the family were drinking in a bar, and one of the guys said to me, "Frankie, you know you're hot all over. You shouldn't be in Miami. People know you here. You have to leave. You have to go somewhere, a remote area, where nobody would know you, so you can cool off for a while." My response was, "Where am I going to go? I can't go to Philly. I can't go to New York. I can't go to Chicago. Where am I going to go? I know I can't stay here in Miami." So he went out to his car and he came in with a map. He opened up the map right there on the bar where we were drinking. In fact, by this time we are drinking pretty heavy. Then he said, "Close your eyes. Throw your hand down, and wherever it lands, that's where you've got to go." Hmmmm, I thought, "That sounds good." Sure enough, I closed my alcohol filled eyes, raised my hand high in the air above the bar, pointed my finger downward, and slammed it right onto Portland, Maine. Old Orchard Beach, to be specific.

What was Old Orchard Beach? It was a resort town where you could hear a pin drop in the winter time, but in the summer it is their season. Bars are open everywhere, and many Canadian people flock there. It was truly the ideal place.

Next I had to take on a new identity. The following day I visited a Catholic Clergy store with the intent of becoming a priest. Surely no one would suspect a priest! I proceeded to purchase a complete priestly attire, with the collar and black shirt and all that goes with it. Then I went to Western Union and sent myself a telegram saying: "Father Jerome Clibbanoff is to report to the Portland, Maine area to resume a position in the church as one of our priests." My thinking was, in case I was stopped along the way, this would verify my new identity. All the way to Maine I dressed as a priest and traveled as a man of the cloth. I was Father Jerome Clibbanoff traveling to Old Orchard Beach.

With my connections I could make myself to be whoever I chose to be, complete with a fictitious name, bogus social security card and number. We used to make fake social security cards by the boxes. Driver's licenses too, but you need to remember back then they did not have pictures on them, only the name. So actually, I could be anybody I wanted to be. Not only did they not have pictures back then, but they didn't have NCIC either. What's NCIC? The National Crime Information Center of the Federal Government. Technology today lets them know who you are, and this would not have been so easy. At the time I was involved in crime, they did not have the resources that are in place today, so I could be anybody I wanted to be, and basically do anything I wanted to do; believe me, I took full advantage of it.

Chapter 9

The Arrest

After arriving in Old Orchard Beach, Maine, all my illegal funds were expended, and basically I was broke, so I began to search for a job. I found work as a cook in a place called Seaside Hotel and Resort. The owner was originally from Sweden. His name was Mr. Hodeen. He was a wonderful human being, both he and his wife. They treated me like a son. They knew me only by my new identity, Jerome Clibanoff. So Jerome Clibanoff became the cook at the Seaside Hotel and Resort for Mr Hodeen, and life went on.

Eventually, the FBI located me when I called my cousin Louie on a payphone. Judy and I saw the same payphone a couple of years ago. It is still there, but the Seaside Hotel and Resort has become a new hotel. Let me tell you how it happened. I called Louie on the pay-phone and he says, "You know, it's so hot down here. You better stay right where you're at. The heat is here. It's so hot. Over 100 degrees or more here." What he was actually saying to me was that the FBI is all over the place looking for me, tailing my family, and doing everything they could to get a lead on me. That is what he was really saying to me in that message. "Yeah, Jerry, stay where you're at, it is just too hot here." So I hung up, and immediately the phone rang back. Not thinking, I picked it up and the operator said, "Sir, you owe 10 cents more on your call." I told her I was out of change, and she asked me if it would be alright to re-verse the charge. I said, "Yeah, just tell my cousin that Jerry's reversing 10 cents. Just reverse the 10 cent charge."

It took only two weeks for the FBI to get that phone record. This is what they later told me. Who would re-verse 10 cents from Old Orchard Beach, Maine, to a Louie Palermo? Well, it didn't take a rocket scientist to figure that one out. The FBI sent my file up to Port-land, and six agents from the FBI rushed into Old Or-chard Beach. It was right after July the 4th. They walked around with a photo of me, asking everyone, "Did you ever see this man? Ever see this guy? Ever see this man?" Everybody answered, "No, no, no." Then came this 15 year-old kid coming down the street. One of the agents stopped him and asked, "You ever see this guy?" He looked at the photo and said, "Yeah, yeah, that's Jerry. Jerry works down at the Seaside Hotel. He's the cook down there." And that is how they found me.

It must have been 7:30 or 8:00 in the morning, and I was working the grill. There were four waitresses on duty, and I was the only cook. About 30 to 40 hungry people filled the dining room. The kitchen was in the back, so I couldn't really see anything going on in the front. I had a hot plate line where I kept putting the prepared food for pick up. I kept ringing the bell for the waitresses to come and pick up the food, ringing the bell, ringing the bell. I wondered, "Where are they? Get this food out of here." Little did I know, or even suspect, that the FBI had cleared the whole building.

Everyone, including employees, were quickly and quietly escorted outside. I had no idea this was taking place. I turned my back on the grill, and three agents rushed in the back, and three rushed in from the front with their guns drawn and pointing directly at me shouting, "FBI! DON'T MOVE OR WE WILL KILL YOU!" It's a good thing I wasn't armed, because they meant what they said. They would have surely killed me that morning. It is only by the grace of God that I am alive today. Then Mr. Hodeen comes running in and he's pushing the agents out of the way and screaming in his thick Swedish accent, "No! No! That is my Jerry! You have the wrong man!" One thing you do not do is interfere with the FBI on an arrest bust. Several of the agents rushed toward him and threw him against the wall with such force that he bounced off and then fell down hard. Hardened criminal that I was, this was one of the saddest things I had ever seen in my life. I do not like to even talk about it. He was down on the ground with FBI guns pointing at him. He kept looking up with big tears in his eyes seeking an answer from me. I had to tell him, "Mr. Hodeen, they have the right man. I have lied to you, I deceived you on purpose. I have betrayed your trust."

That is what the devil does best. He is the betrayer and will make you betray others. He does not care about you or anyone, he is the destroyer. John 10:10 tells us, "The thief cometh not, but for to steal, and to kill, and to destroy: I [Jesus] am come that they might have life, and that they might have it more abundantly." Satan will try to destroy your family, your marriage, and your children. His intent is to destroy everything that is holy between you and a Holy God, if you let him. Only by the grace of God, it doesn't happen. The Lord once told Paul in 2 Corinthians 12:9, "My grace is sufficient for thee," and He meant that for us too.

God's grace is far reaching. It is interesting to note here, that after I was saved and out of prison sharing my testimony, God showed me extra grace again. I was doing a service in Hermon, Maine, at a church by the name of Hermon Baptist Church. The Pastor was Garnet Chute. I gave my testimony to maybe four or five hundred people there. At the close of the service, Pastor Chute asked Judy and I to greet the people at the back of the church. We were standing there shaking hands and greeting all the beautiful people, and a lady approached me. Instead of shaking my hand, I got a big hug. She was about fifty years-old, and as she hugged me, she said to me, "It is so wonderful of you to be here, and by the way, my uncle told me to please send his best regards to you. He is so proud of what you are now." "Your uncle?" I questioned her. "Who is your uncle?" She said, "His name is George O'Keith." I thought about it and repeated the name back to her, telling her the only O'Keith I knew of was the one that was involved in the Boston robbery of the Brinks. Spec O'Keith was involved in the famous Brinks robbery in the 50's when over a million and a half dollars were stolen from Brinks. That is the only one I know of. I do not think I know your uncle.

She firmly replied, "Yes, you do know him, because he was one of the FBI agents that arrested you at Old Orchard Beach." Wow, I was stunned. I was shocked. Amazed, I reaffirmed to her, "You mean he was one of the agents that stormed into the kitchen and arrested me back then?" She said, "Yes, and he has heard all about your evangelism and all that you are now doing. He is very proud of you." Needless to say, I was floored and amazed at the same time. This is the grace of God, to bring this man back into my life under such different circumstances many years later. The pastor also commented about what a marvelous God we serve. One of the men who arrested me, now retired from the FBI, is still a part of my life. Awesome. It shows me every step of our life is orchestrated and planned by God for our good.

Once in custody, they took me to the county jail where I was locked up close to four months trying to fight extradition with my court appointed attorney. They extradited me anyway. I was sent back to New York City to stand trial. I remained locked up at the Metropolitan Correctional Facility in New York City for eighteen long months.

During the first trial, twenty-three witnesses were called and came forward for the government. They only had to do one thing: take the stand and identify me by pointing and saying, "That is the man, that is the man, that is the man."

After enough times of that, the judge finally called the trial to a halt. I still had a court appointed attorney, because I had no money. I was no longer in a position to call on anybody for money due to my precarious situation. The judge put an end to the trial right in the middle of it. He told my court appointed attorney, "You go down and tell that kid he has one opportunity to throw the towel in. Tell him to quit. I will try to help him, but if he doesn't, he has enough charges to get himself 30 long prison years."

My attorney came down and told me exactly what the judge said. Well, I was Mr. Tough guy. I wouldn't let anybody stop me, no one or no thing. I love nobody. I care for nobody, not even for myself or my future. Defiantly, I proceeded to instruct my attorney to tell the "ole man" judge that I am not throwing in no towel! Yes, I called the judge an "ole man," and I really didn't care what might happen to me. I continued, "Tell him to bring it on. I'm not guilty of nothing." Obviously taken aback, my attorney replied, "Oh, I can't go and tell the judge that." Angrily, I retorted, "Well, if you don't go tell him now, I will tell him when I get back in court." With a look of unbelief at my stupidity, my mouthpiece continued to try to reason with me. Looking at me to give me one last opportunity to reconsider, he once again questioned, "You want me to go tell him that?" I firmly replied, "Go tell him that." Sure enough, he went and told him exactly what I said.

You know how long the jury was out? Twelve minutes! How many people are on a jury? Twelve...that is a minute a piece. It took only twelve minutes' time. Presumptuously, I am sitting there watching them parade back in, and I egotistically look at my lawyer and say, "This looks like a good sign." He looked at me as if to say, "What planet are you from?" They found me guilty. The judge said, "Bring the big shot up here."

Sure enough, I went up before that judge, and he gave me thirty years in prison without blinking an eye.

Next, they sent me to New Jersey where more charges were pending. The federal detention center in Mays Landing was my next home for awhile. That jail just closed a couple of years ago. This time while I was there, I had enough sense to realize they were likely to sentence me to life or something similar. I wasn't charged with any murders, or I would still be in prison.

Truthfully, if they had given me everything I deserved for the crimes I had done, there would not be enough life sentences to pay for it. What I am telling you is, that in reality, they could have given me 300 to 400 years, and sad to say, it would have been just punishment for the crimes. Instead, I got away with so many bad things I had done. A lot of terrible crimes were never addressed, they were just missed. At the next trial, under title 20 of U.S. code, I plead guilty. This time I was sentenced to another thirty-five years on top of the other thirty originally given. That brought me to a total sentence of sixty-five years in prison. They did not want me back out on the street ever again. Eighteen months I stayed in Jersey, and then I was shipped to the Federal Penitentiary in Lewisburg, Pennsylvania.

This was Frankie's hideout while working at the Seaside Hotel and Resort in Old Orchard Beach, Maine.

The pay phone in Old Orchard Beach Frankie used to call his cousin Louie. The FBI tracked where he was hiding through the family's phone record.

Chapter 10

My Heavenly Visit in Hell

The first two years in Lewisburg I was kept in solitary confinement. Let me explain a little about solitary confinement in those days. At 4:00 to 4:30 every afternoon, you got a rug to sleep on, yes a rug. There was no pillow and no mattress. At 7:00 the next morning, they took the rug up. You were in solitary, and you were confined. They also had another thing in Lewisburg. It was a yellow line down the hall that led to the mess hall. You didn't dare step over the yellow line, because when I was in prison, the guards could hit you, and they would. I don't know what prison is like today. I don't want to go back there and see, but I hear them tell about boom boxes, televisions, mommy sends candy, and basically, you get whatever you want. You can even tell the guards off and nothing happens. It didn't happen that way with me. I don't understand this today. We're in a different day and hour. Prison is not the prison I used to know.

We went back and ministered at the prison in Maine recently. They had a garden outside, a cafeteria so clean you could eat off the floor, telephones, computers, and gymnastics. My wife posed the question after observing these amenities in the prison. She said, "Honey, you think they like it here?" Sixty-seven people got saved that day, by the way. My reply was, "There could be a very good possibility that they do." It was never that way while I was in prison. Things have changed drastically, and the prison population keeps growing and growing. When you consider there are 2.7 million people in our prisons in the United States of America, 375,000 of them women, leaving 1.5 million children without parents at home because they are incarcerated, you have to admit there is something drastically wrong in America. I'm giving you straight statistics that I know for sure. The only thing that can reverse these alarming statistics is a spiritual awakening that changes the hearts of men and women of every race, color and creed.

Anyway, while I was there, I wanted to die. I got transferred from there down to Atlanta. Right about that time Brother Ralph from Glen Haven Baptist Church was coming in. Bob Harrington had just come in to minister with a music group called the Lefevres. I took a liking to Brother Ralph because he had a love of God in his heart for people. I was impressed by that. I remember writing him a couple of times, and do you know, he wrote me back. He even came to see me when I was not even saved. He wasn't there when I got saved, but he planted the seed.

Let me tell you a little about this federal prison in Atlanta. When I arrived in Atlanta, I didn't know what tough guys were until I met them in that prison. There were ten murders my first year there. One guy got his skull crushed when he was hit in the head by a rock in a sock thrown by another feuding inmate. I watched one prisoner murdered with a homemade knife stuck straight through his heart, because he owed the other inmate two packs of Pall Mall cigarettes. Another one got strangled in the third tier over a homosexual affair. They threw one guy from the fifth tier, 120 feet down. It took a brush and a hose to clean all the body parts up. That was Atlanta, and that was what it was like living with tough guys.

Later, I did get saved while I was in my cell. It was nighttime, between 9:00 and 10:00 pm. In Atlanta between the hour of 9:00 to 10:00 each night, they would play soft piped music throughout the dorms of the prison. Brother Frankie knew he was in some serious, serious trouble. The music would play. I was in my cell this night, and I wanted to die. I was so lonely. Nobody wrote to me. I had no family, no visits, nothing. You know what I knew? I was going to die in prison. I was going to DIE IN PRISON, and I was wanting it to come soon.

This particular night, the music was playing, and I took the pillow and I kept pushing and pushing my face into that pillow to smoother myself, because I wanted to die. I had no hope, no hope whatsoever. Then a song came on. A slow song with two guys singing. Their names are Simon and Garfunkel. The song they were singing on the night I was going to kill myself was called "Bridge Over Troubled Water."

The next thing I knew, I saw myself in a cesspool. I saw it with the pillow over my face while I was trying to kill myself. I saw myself in this dark cesspool sinking down and down and down. I was seeing myself descending right into the pits of hell. Then all of a sudden, while trying to kill myself by pressing my face in the pillow with "Bridge Over Troubled Water" playing, miraculously I saw a hand reach down to grab my hand to save me from that cesspool of hell. When that happened, I literally felt something touch me. At the moment He touched me, these words came out of my mouth, "God??? God, do you love me? Do you really love me? I'm dying here, God. I'm going to die." Then I heard a voice speak to me, "Let me tell you something." Now when I tell people that I heard a voice, they say, "You didn't really hear a voice." I reply, "Do you know why I heard a voice? Because God is sovereign." Do you know what that means? He's God and He will do whatever he wants to do to get your attention. In His mercy and my time of need, I heard a voice speaking to me audibly, saying, "I sent my Son to die for you, Frankie." I fell on my face in that cold, dark prison cell, and I don't know how long I was down there on my knees confessing everything I had done over the past years. It took me awhile to confess it all, but I was seeking the mercy and forgiveness of the Lord Jesus Christ.

I knew when I got up that Brother Frankie would never be the same again. First thing I did was to go and get me a Bible. From that night on my heart's desire was to study and learn the word of God.

My job inside the federal prison was working at a cotton mill. Nine times I went for parole, and each time they denied me. The Mafia mobsters locked up with me used to make fun of me, laughing and cursing or mocking me.

It did not take long for word to get back to my father what had happened to me. They told my father, "Oh, that son of yours is now carrying a Bible and talking about Jesus." I was the joke of the family. They all laughed and made fun of me, the big time gangster who now has a crutch. They considered it a crutch that I carried a Bible and relied on Jesus. "He's got a Bible in his hand for a crutch to carry around."

The tenth time I went before the parole board, I was paroled. When I came out of prison, I stayed on parole for twelve and one-half long years, checking in with them every time I breathed. I could not move or do anything without their permission. During this time however, I stuck to my heart's intent to learn God's word and enrolled in Bible college to study the word of God.

One thing that I knew, I was never going back to that kind of life ever again. That was determined in my heart, and there was no turning back. Did you ever hear that expression, "Don't burn all your bridges behind you?" Well, let me tell you something, Brother Frankie burned every bridge behind him, so that I would have no where to retreat to. My advice to you is to burn every bridge of ungodliness behind you and go straight forward for Jesus Christ from this moment on.

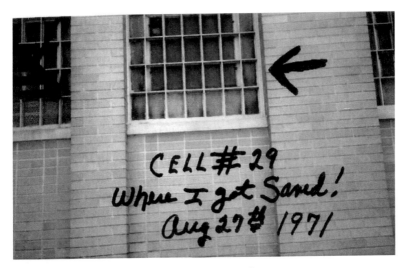

The prison cell where the great transformation took place
August 27, 1971.

Atlanta Federal Prison in Atlanta, Georgia, where Frankie spent
15 years out of a 65-year prison term.

Chapter 11

Bible College

When I came out of prison, after spending fifteen years in that horrible place, the first thing I did was sign up for Bible college in Lynchburg, Virginia. Yes, I had to get permission from the parole board. Even though I had served fifteen years of my sentence, I was still paroled for twelve and one-half more years after they released me back into society.

The reason I chose to go to Jerry Falwell's school was from a friend's suggestion that it was a good school and a good place to go. However, the real reason I went was because I wanted to study the word of God to show myself approved unto God. Now God is first and foremost in my life, and so I wanted to learn as much as possible about the word of God. That was my motivating factor for attending Bible college, and still holds true today.

In the course of my studies, I met a friend by the name of Giuseppe Parisi. Giuseppe was Italian, like I am, and from Sicily too. He was married with three lovely young daughters. Giuseppe and I were both in Bible college at the same time. We each paid our own way in Bible college and worked hard in order to do it. But there was something different about Giuseppe Parisi, because he could barely speak English. I always used to tease him and say, "Hey Joe, you talk like you've got a loaf of bread in your mouth. Learn some English, will ya!"

Speaking in his broken English, he once asked me, "Uh, Frankie, uh, tell me your testimony. How you got saved with the Jesus man?" Quite honestly, at that time, I was ashamed of my past, and it was with great reluctance that I told him. My only condition was that it must stay between us only; I did not want it to get around. It wasn't until years later that the Lord really prompted me to start sharing this testimony. So I told him about who I was, what I did, what happened, how it happened, and how I had been saved. The next thing I know, Joe blurts out, "Why, you, you're a trophy of God's marvelous grace." Frantically waving my hands at him, I replied, "Joe, don't say that. It's like you're putting me on a pedestal. Please don't say that, Joe." Excitedly, he exclaimed, "Oh no, no, no. I got to tell

everybody! You're a trophy of God's marvelous grace."
Thus, he began telling everybody in the school that I
was a trophy of God's marvelous grace. In the hall-
ways, in the classrooms, wherever we would cross
paths, he would exclaim, "Do you see that man over
there? That is Frankie Palermo. He is a trophy of God's
marvelous grace. Frankie, come over here and tell
them about your story."

He was really putting me on the spot. Once we went
to a local restaurant together. After the waitress served
us our coffee, I warned him, "Joe? Remember what I
said and keep your mouth shut. Don't say anything to
anyone today, OK?" When the waitress returned, the
next thing I knew, he blurted out, "Do you know who
this man is? This man is a trophy of God's marvelous
grace. Frankie, tell her your story. Tell her your story
Frankie!" The waitress looked down at me half inter-
ested and said hurriedly, "What's your story, buddy?"
So, I began to share just a little bit about myself. This
happened every single time we went somewhere. I remember one time we were in the cafeteria, but on different sides of the room, Guiseppe stood up on one of
the chairs and screamed out, while waving and pointing his finger at me, "Do you see that man over there?
He's a trophy of God's marvelous grace. Frankie! Come
here and tell them your story."

When I used to see him coming, I would hide in the
bathroom. I hid under tables and used to tell him, "The

next time you do it, I'm going to get you! You understand that?" "Frankie, you're a man of God's marvelous grace. You're a trophy of the grace of God." Often I think of this. It was kind of funny back then, but truthfully, Brother Parisi was right. You are reading about a man that is a trophy of God's marvelous mercy and grace. Little did I realize it then, how right he was. We are all trophies of God's marvelous grace because of the shed blood of Jesus. I am not ashamed of my testimony anymore, only the things that I did in my past life. But I am now well aware I am the righteousness of God in Christ Jesus, and He has removed my past from me as far as the East is from the West. He does not remember them anymore, and neither do I. That gangster, Frankie "D" Palermo, is dead. He died in prison. I have been born again, a new creation in Christ. Old things have passed away, and all things have become new.

Frankie presenting his testimony in visual effects at the community building in East Machais, Maine. He has done this multiple times in other places as well, with many souls coming to Christ.

2010 Lifebuilders Conference in Wimauma, FL. Frankie was one of the guest speakers. About 1200 men were present. Frankie received his first standing ovation.

Chapter 12

My Beautiful Wife Judy

While we are talking about new, not only did the Lord make me brand new, but He introduced me to my helpmeet, Judy. Many people ask us how and where did we meet, so I want to take a moment here and share with you the most wonderful woman and minister of the Gospel that I know.

I first met Judy when she was sharing the cell block next to mine! Just a joke, of course. Truthfully, it was on an evening service, in August of 1989, when I walked into the sanctuary of Evangel Tabernacle where Judy was the pianist. She was sitting there looking more beautiful than I can express to you here. We spoke briefly after the service, and then we went our separate ways.

Judy's pastor had invited me, a Baptist trained minister, to speak in their Pentecostal church. Judy was less than impressed, to say the least. In fact she later informed her pastor, Robert Wiley, that it would be alright with her if he never asked me back again. Judy later told me I may have called it preaching, but she termed it more appropriately, boring.

It was later that I was drawn back to Evangel Tabernacle, and it just so happened, Judy was the preacher for that Sunday evening. What a preacher she was! I complemented her on a job well done, and actually told her she had preached better than most men I had heard.

Not long after that, I found myself visiting Town and Country Church of God on a Sunday night. Pastor James Scott was the officiating pastor, and Rev. Larry Mason was the guest speaker for that service. The Holy Ghost baptism was the topic, and after much resistance, I found myself at the altar kneeling when I was filled with the mighty Holy Ghost.

Now it is my testimony everywhere I go, that if you do not have the gift of the Holy Ghost, you are cheating yourself. Returning to Evangel Tabernacle Church, where Judy was a member, Pastor Wiley licensed and commissioned me as an Evangelist that Sunday morning. Judy played "The Family of God," and all the congregation joined in and gave me the right hand of fellowship. It was an anointed moment, and I was charged up and ready to go. I was gloriously sent out by Pastor Wiley and the Evangel Tabernacle Church, leaving Judy at the piano with her not knowing I had an eye for her.

In December 1989, Judy relocated to Scottshill, Tennessee, after living in the Greater Tampa Bay area for the last twenty-plus years. Judy later expressed to me what a change it was to her. Leaving the palm trees, the warm weather, the beautiful white sandy seashores, for the cold, frigid weather in Tennessee.

On a Sunday evening in 1994, while Judy was returning home from church, she noticed the voice mail notification flashing on her phone. I had left her a voice mail after some difficulty in locating her number. The operator had given me the area code, but I was unaware that there were two different area codes for Tennessee at that time. Well, the first one got me nowhere, but I was determined to talk to the anointed pianist that had originally caught my eye some time back. So I finally got the correct area code and left her a voice mail to call me.

After Judy returned my call, we began to talk on a regular basis. The calls became more frequent as time went on. Judy and I never really dated. Our courtship was by phone and mail. We never went to a movie together or even dinner. We never caressed or kissed each other until we exchanged our wedding vows in Gainesville, Florida, on December 8, 1995.

People find our story a bit amusing, as we never slept together before marriage to see if we were compatible, as the common wave of immorality dictates today. It is like this, when God is the author of the partnership, He will make everything beautiful in His time.

Judy and I had a mutual attraction and love for each other that became increasingly obvious to us both as we continued the long distance relationship. She was made aware of my past in organized crime, as well as my years of incarceration. Judy confesses, however, that the one thing I did not share with her was my age. All I told her was that I moved right into my criminal career immediately after an honorable discharge from military service during the Korean war.

She finally figured out that I was sixty-two years old. She is somewhat younger, but that did not deter us. God had brought us together, and we were meant to be.

However, it was not that simple for her parents, my new in-laws. They did not like me one bit. It was their opinion I was still a gangster, and they wanted nothing to do with their daughter being connected to me. It took eight months before they received me into their family.

John 8:36 says, "If the Son therefore shall make you free, ye shall be free indeed." And that is exactly what happened.

Judy's parents are already in heaven, but if they were here, they would tell you the same as Joseph Perissi, that Frankie Palermo is truly a trophy of God's marvelous grace. Frankie is carrying a different weapon today, it is called the Sword of the Spirit, the word of God.

For the past seventeen years, at this book's writing, Judy and I have traveled the country sharing the good news of Jesus Christ wherever we were invited. We have ministered in almost every denomination, crossing barriers that only the Holy Spirit can break down. We have gone into many state and federal prisons and several juvenile detention centers with a mighty moving of the power of God to save and deliver. In fact, during the past seventeen years of ministry, we have seen over sixteen thousand come to Christ in repentance of their sins.

Our motto has become, "souls are our business, our only business." Judy and I do everything together. Where you see one, you see the other. Both of us consider it to be a tremendous blessing that God brought us to each other. What He does, He does perfectly. She is a complement to my ministry, and I like to think I am a complement to hers. We work together, colaborers in the Lord, committed to the Lord first and then to each other. As Ecclesiastes 4:12 says, "A three fold cord is not quickly broken." We give God all the glory, all the honor, and all the praise for allowing our paths to cross. He united us as one, placed us in the King's service, and to this day we are actively involved in ministry, serving God together, waiting for His soon return.

Frankie and Judy renewed their wedding vows on January 31, 2011, on their 15th anniversary. The reason for their happy marriage is because Christ is the center of their lives.

This photo is of Frankie with Pastor Nagele and his sons posing as
gangsters at Church of God in Brockway, PA.

Frankie ministering at Church of God in Mayfield, Kentucky.

Chapter 13

The Life of an Evangelist

When I was still in my life of crime back in the Miami beach area with all of my mob friends, before fleeing to Old Orchard Beach, we had a preacher approach us. He was a street evangelist. Now, many years later, I was then unaware that I would one day stand in the shoes of this man of God. Here is what happened.

It was Miami Beach, and we had been literally drinking all night until about three or four in the morning, until we crashed. Next morning, we got up for breakfast and coffee and headed for the beach where we would spend the rest of the day drinking and partying again. There was about twenty to twenty-five of us this particular day, with a few kegs of beer in tote and some bottles of whiskey to chase it with. Of course we had girls with us, we referred to them as broads in those days, wearing bikinis and little to nothing in swimwear. We were there to party and have a good time, and that is what we thought we did.

Around noontime, in the midst of all this revelry, we noticed a man coming our way. He was alone and looked to be about 5'4" or so, and maybe one hundred thirty pounds. He was short in stature with wire rim glasses propped halfway down his nose and a small book in his hand. This man walked right into the middle of us and announced, "I have good news for you today." He continued on with us wondering what he was doing. He said, "Did you know the wages of sin is death? Did you know that? But, the gift of God is eternal life to anyone who will believe in the Lord Jesus Christ." Then he proceeded to really get started preaching, and he preached, and he preached. He was preaching salvation and delivering it in Pentecostal style with spit flying and finger pointing.

We were laughing at him and finding it quite amusing. We were telling him to preach on, and in general mocking him. Then it began to get serious. He started saying, "Where the worm dieth not and the fire is never quenched. Did you know there is no escape from hell once you go there? You will burn there forever!" He kept on, and it got more serious, "You will never see your loved ones again. You will be doomed to outer darkness for eternity." We began to feel the flames licking at our feet. Everyone became very uncomfortable.

A couple of the guys murmured, "Let's get rid of this guy so we can go on with our party." Another one commented, "We ought to drag him out into the ocean and see if he can swim. We can take him into the deep and leave him, if he can't swim, too bad." And they would laugh and mock while devising other scenarios to try to silence the truth from penetrating their false security of alcohol and women.

One of our guys finally stood up and said, "I am getting tired of this guy!" Then he proceeded to pick up a handful of sand and throw it right in the preacher's face. With sand in his eyes, that little short preacher reeled back, somewhat stunned, and shook his head. He pulled out the handkerchief with which he had been wiping the spit from his preaching, but this time cleaned his face, eyes and glasses. Then he turned right back to us and proceeded to start preaching again.

He said, "Did you know the wages of sin is death? And that is what you are facing today. Did you know if you sow the wind, you will inherit the whirlwind, and some of you are reaping the whirlwind now. God is not mocked. Whatsoever a man sows, that will he reap." He continued preaching the reality of sin and the consequences right to us.

Next, one of the girls walked up to him and spit right in his face. It covered his glasses and much of his face. As the saliva ran down, he calmly pulled out the handkerchief again and wiped it off, this time putting his glasses into his pocket. All of a sudden, he comes right back into our rowdy crowd, this time with his book open, preaching the Holy Word of God with fire. "You are facing certain death today. I am warning you, because the wages of sin is death. Hear what I am telling you. You will inherit hell; there is only one way out. Repent! Repent!" He was loudly and boldly proclaiming truth.

One of the guys said, "We are tired of this, somebody needs to knock him out." That was all it took for one of the bigger guys to stand up and pop the preacher right in the face, knocking him down for a moment. He was struck so hard it looked as if he had been thrown. Laying in the sand, we heard him groaning from the blow to his jaw.

Amazed as we were, we see him start to get up again, clutching his Bible in his hand. After standing upright, he takes out his hanky to wipe the blood from his chin. Then he opens the Bible and walks right into the midst of us again and lays out the Word to us with power! He said, "I am going to tell you one more time that the wages of sin is death, and everyone of you are heading for death, repent!"

There is no more laughter from us, we are fed up with this preacher and ready to severely hurt him to shut him up. Laughter had turned to hate, and we were just about to pour it out on him when the police arrived.

Two patrol officers showed up and came running to find out what was happening. They pull the preacher back and stand in front of us so we could not get at him. They begin asking us what was the problem. Sad thing is, they arrest the preacher for inciting a riot and take him away in handcuffs. They told him he had no right coming down to the crowded beach, preaching and causing a problem. They said preaching is for the church, as they loaded him into the back of the squad car and took him downtown.

We laughed and laughed at what we did to that street preacher the rest of the day. But today I look back on it, and I see myself in that preacher as clear as can be. Many times as I reminisce about this incident, I think to myself how that man was preaching right to Frankie. I never knew at that time that I would one day be standing in the shoes of the man of God and someone would spit on me as I preached. Somebody would try to punch me out, another would kick me in my shins, while yet another would curse me and ridicule me and mock me. Even some of my own family would laugh and make sport of my faith. Yet, like the street preacher in Miami, I continue to pick up my cross and endure persecution for my Lord's sake, telling people everywhere, to "Come follow Me," just like Jesus said. I thank God that the man of God had the backbone to come and plant that seed in my life, that the wages of sin is death, but the gift of God is eternal life.

A couple of years ago, we were doing a revival in Canada. It was a Friday, Saturday and Sunday night revival. We had ministered in Canada prior to this with many revivals. People would get saved, and there had never been a problem. During this particular revival, the first night I preached, twenty-three people got saved! The very next day, the Canadian police took me into custody and arrested me as an undesirable in their country. They told me I could not stay in Canada because I was an undesirable. Their orders were for me to get out of Canada, and they meant it. Promptly they escorted me back to the border. Judy got in touch with the church where we were in revival, and they tried to intervene, but could not. The church was in an uproar over my arrest, since I had been free from crime for many years now.

Again the officers sternly reiterated that I was not welcome in Canada due to my long record of criminal activity, and in no uncertain terms, demanded I leave their country immediately. Precious Judy tearfully requested permission to take me back to where we were staying in order to collect our belongings. "Absolutely not," was their firm reply. One last desperate time she asked them if she could drive me back across the border into America. "He's got to walk across the bridge," was their cruel retort. It was only maybe about a block from the Canadian customs to the U.S. customs, but they made me walk over the bridge. Their last words to me still ring in my mind, "If you come back here anymore we will arrest you and next time keep you." Slowly and painfully I began to walk that bridge. It seemed like a million miles walking alone back to America. As I walked across that bridge, I felt so many things in my heart that day, hurt, shame, and my thoughts were, "What have I done? What's going on here?" As I walked, I started to pray and cry. I couldn't help it, the way I felt in my heart. I said, "Lord, why? Why?" I kept asking. Half way there I heard the voice of the Lord on the bridge speak to me. He said, "Did I not tell you when I called you to be an evangelist, that you had to pick up your cross and follow Me, and did I promise it was going to be easy? No. But I promised you I would never leave you or forsake you, and now, you're not walking on the bridge alone today, because I'm walking with you." That's what He said to me half way across that bridge. When I got to the other side, the Americans took me into custody and held me another 45 minutes. Then they let me go.

Last year we tried to go into Canada again. I was still not thinking straight by attempting this. We had our passports and all documents. They got us again, but at a different bridge. This time they made it very clear. They said, "You see this form? It says that if we see you again, we are going to arrest you immediately, and you will not come out of Canada any more. Sign it now and get out of Canada." Well, I had to sign it. They searched my car, my briefcase and all my belongings, then they escorted us right out of Canada. They took me into custody on the American side again. So, we still cannot go to Canada to this day, ending the Canadian ministry trips for us. We are thankful for the five to seven revivals we were able to do in Canada before this.

When I was 62 years old, I went and filed for Social Security benefits while Judy waited outside. Inside the Social Security office, there was a young government employee assisting me. She was typing in my social security number while I filed a claim for my benefits. She stopped in the middle of her typing and said, "Can I ask you a personal question?" I said, "Yeah, what is it?" She said, "Where have you been for 20 years?" I said, "What?" She asked again, "Where have you been for 20 years?" I said, "Why do you ask such a question?" She said, "Because I see 20 years of nothing on your social security. You're only going to get $327 a month." Well, I was excited, because to me that was a lot of money. I was so elated about the $327, I guess I did not respond quick enough. So she asked again, "Where did you say you have been?" I said, "I'll tell you where I've been. Fourteen and a half of those years I spent in prisons. And the other amount of time I spent running from every law enforcement agency you can think of."

Startled and dumbfounded, she just blankly stared at me not knowing quite how to react. Later on in my ministry, the Lord showed me Galatians 6:7. "Be not deceived; God is not mocked: for whatsoever a man soweth, that shall he also reap." And the Lord showed me this, "Don't you remember all those years when you were stealing and robbing and making all that money? That's the seed you sowed. It's the seed you planted. Sure your sins are forgiven, but you sowed that seed." And guess what, it was harvest time. The chickens came home to roost. Three hundred and twenty-seven dollars. Thank God He restores, and I did not have to stay that way. He has blessed and continues to bless us in abundance as we travel the continent proclaiming His glory and goodness.

Chapter 14

Closing Thoughts

I look back over the 39 years of this ministry we call No Boundaries Ministries. I am so grateful I have a beautiful wife who has ministered along with me for seventeen years at this writing. During those seventeen years, we've had over 16,500 souls saved.

Why do we go back into the prisons? We go back because that's where we need to go, and that's where God sends us. We have a good turn out every time, and people always get saved. Souls are our business, our only business. That is what No Boundaries Ministries represents. Souls are our only business. Until the day I graduate to Glory, I will proclaim His good news, the Gospel of Jesus Christ. Jesus Christ saves and delivers too! Yes, I am a trophy of that marvelous grace of God, and I boast in the Lord for all He has done. The beautiful thing is that all this is available to whosoever will.

I invite you to hear the Lord speaking to you today and become a trophy of His grace too. I am happy to help you, just pray this prayer, and afterward write to me at the address below. I want to hear from you.

Pray this prayer:

Father, in Jesus Name, I want forgiveness of my sins. I recognize my need for a Savior; I cannot do it alone. Please forgive me, wash me clean in the Blood of Jesus. Father, I believe in my heart that Jesus died for me and was raised from the dead on my behalf, and I now proclaim Him as my Lord and Savior. In Jesus Name, Thank You, Amen.

Now if you prayed that prayer, please let me know so Judy and I can pray for you too.

Write to us at:
No Boundaries Ministries
P O Box 14931
Bradenton, FL 34280

My prayer for you is found in Ephesians 1:15-23:

"Wherefore I also, after I heard of your faith in the Lord Jesus, and love unto all the saints, Cease not to give thanks for you, making mention of you in my prayers; That the God of our Lord Jesus Christ, the Father of glory, may give unto you the spirit of wisdom and revelation in the knowledge of him: The eyes of your understanding being enlightened; that ye may know what is the hope of his calling, and what the riches of the glory of his inheritance in the saints, And what is the exceeding greatness of his power to us-ward who believe, according to the working of his mighty power, Which he wrought in Christ, when he raised him from the dead, and set him at his own right hand in the heavenly places, Far above all principality, and power, and might, and dominion, and every name that is named, not only in this world, but also in that which is to come: And hath put all things under his feet, and gave him to be the head over all things to the church, Which is his body, the fullness of him that filleth all in all."

Amen and Amen.

And it shall come to pass, that whosoever shall call on the name of the Lord shall be saved.
— Acts 2:21